Go of my Heart

a prayer book
for youth

compiled and edited by
Connie Wlaschin Ruhlman

I dedicate this book
to my dad, Bernard A. Wlaschin,
who taught me how to pray,
and to the Marycrest Franciscans,
who helped me deepen that prayerlife
and gave me the opportunity to teach others.

Living the Good News, Inc.
a division of The Morehouse Group
Editorial Offices
600 Grant Street, Suite 400
Denver, CO 80203

James R. Creasey, Publisher

Project Editor: Dirk deVries

Cover Design and Layout: Val Price

Printed in the United States of America.

The scripture quotations used herein are from the New Revised Standard Version, ©1989 by the Division of Christian Education of the National Council of Churches of Christ in the USA. Used by permission.

ISBN 1-889108-39-1

Contents

Introduction

A prayerbook for teenagers is not a new or novel idea. But prayers for teenagers written *by teenagers* for use throughout the *liturgical year,* based on *scripture* and using *inclusive images* to address God— *that's* a novel idea!

How did this idea move from the "dream" stage to this published volume, *God of My Heart?* It started as an assignment in Senior High Theology at St. Patrick's High School in North Platte, Nebraska, where I taught for seventeen years. I asked each student to design and fill a prayerbook with a variety of prayers, "store-bought" and original, free-verse and stylized, and several using the form now published in this book. In regards to this particular prayer format, I asked my students to:

- ■ find a scripture meaningful to them
- ■ address God in a personal, inclusive way
- ■ write out some meaningful thoughts worth sharing in regard to their chosen scripture
- ■ ask God for help to grow and become aware
- ■ state an action they will do to foster their spiritual growth

One year I had a group of especially fine, faith-filled and moti-vated writers. Due to their enthusiasm, my zeal for the project outran my good sense; I determined to produce, by the end of the year, a book of student prayers that could be used in our school on a daily basis. Our school system always started the day with a com-munal prayer via the intercom, and I thought that students' per-sonal prayers based on scripture would be much better than the "canned" ones we haphazardly gathered.

The class responded well to my earnestness, and I presumed I would photocopy the prayers when the project was completed. As usual, optimism clouded my good sense (perhaps the final demise of many good teaching careers?), and with my teaching schedule, family life and other outside activities, it became a future to-do project, gathering dust in the out basket on my desk. Sound familiar?

A year later, however, I used a hundred of the prayers for a paper in one of my graduate classes. David Thomas, then director of the Regis Adult Learning Program, encouraged me to pursue publication of that paper. I'd never considered that a possibility. Hmmm.

As a Catholic-school teacher, I knew there was both a need and a void when it came to original prayers by teens for teens based on scripture. I also knew that these prayers were authentic, from my students' hearts (motivated somewhat, of course, by a need for a passing grade). So, with David's encouragement, I sent the manuscript to a friend's brother, a Catholic publisher. His youth editor said "Sorry, the prayers don't fit our style." But this kind man did take the manuscript to a youth conference for consideration by other publishers. I was grateful and pleased for the unsolicited exposure, but after six more months passed, and I hadn't heard anything, I thought the project had died a natural death.

At that point, word came from Dirk deVries at **Living the Good News**. He informed me that his company wanted to publish the book as a liturgical prayerbook for teens. Another hurdle: my original dream was to publish a daily prayerbook for and by teens; this liturgical-cycle book was about two hundred and fifteen prayers short of that dream! After lengthy discussion with my husband Joe, and other supportive friends, and after re-reading the students' reflections, I began to see possibilities. A liturgical prayerbook would certainly be a good start, and perhaps, if it proved successful, it might be possible to revive the original dream and publish a book of daily prayers.

I said yes to Dirk's offer and began editing prayers and gathering release forms.

Introduction

And now, four years after its original conception, my dream has become a reality. Who would have imagined it? Dreams do come true!

In your hands you hold the fruit of many months of labor and the insightful ups and downs of a variety of teenagers' faith lives. What a joy to help birth these young authors' works and to realize even more profoundly that the Spirit indeed directs what we often presume to be the happenstance of life and its opportunities for growth. I hope these teenagers' prayers find a warm welcome in the hands of Christian youth who wish to begin and continue a relationship with the God of their hearts.

Leaders/Teachers:

Why would I use this book with my students? Knowing that the prayers were written by teens themselves would first draw my interest. Then I would be eager to explore the inclusive images of God as s/he is addressed in each prayer; any way we can broaden our image of God is a plus. Scripture reflection is also a big attraction. These prayers show that teens are often eager to explore what God's word says in their lives. If you're like me and have taught teenagers for any length of time, you probably have a partially filled shelf of prayerbooks that you've used in your work with them; some have even become like old friends. I hope *God of My Heart* will become one of those friends. Hopefully, it's fresh approach will add thoughtful insights and discussion to both your large and small youth gatherings.

How can this book be used? One obvious way to use *God of My Heart* is for prayer-time at Christian-sponsored teenage functions that follow the liturgical year. It also serves as a personal prayerbook. Beyond that, your youth group could reflect on the given scripture and share their own prayerful reflections. As part of each class, this might intensify the message contained in God's word. You might also brainstorm other possible titles for God and make

God of My Heart

a list that your students find especially meaningful. Future prayer could begin by addressing God in these various ways. Discussing these God-images and their appropriateness in prayer could fill several class periods. The action suggested at the end of each prayer ties together faith and actions; discussion of faith in action as witnessed in our heroes and "sheroes" would be a fine addition to any lesson plan.

Teens:

I hope you find *God of My Heart* fresh and insightful, deepening your prayer life. It is a prayerbook written for teenagers by teenagers...it is a book for you written by your peers.

As a teacher, I am aware that there are several good prayerbooks for your age group on the market, so why this one? It's different. This approach to prayer—the use of scripture, the language for God, the reflections and the suggested actions—might be just what you are looking for when it comes to personal prayer-time, or when it comes to group prayer in your religious education or Sunday school classes.

My wish for you as editor of this book, as a former teacher of some very faith-filled students, is that *God of My Heart* will speak to your heart and become a prayerbook that you use daily. As you pray through the ups and downs of a typical year, use it liturgically and seasonally, or zero in on the theme index (pages 137-142) to deal with what's on your mind at the moment.

I believe these teenager's thoughts, feelings and experiences will speak to you and give you a boost as you strive to understand and deepen your own relationship with God.

Connie Wlaschin Ruhlman

Advent

The Season of Advent

The Incarnation (the union of the divine and the human in the person of Jesus) is an event we've celebrated for almost 2000 years, and each year we eagerly attempt to refocus on God's gift: Jesus. We make that attempt in Advent, the time of preparation and waiting for this gift. Yes, it's true, we often lose the focus, but as Christians we are always drawn back...back to the manger, its generous gift and its stark simplicity.

Our Advent prayers offered here do just that: draw us back to the basics. In these reflections we are able to focus on the simplicity of the manger, the awesomeness of Incarnation. We gain fresh insights into what it means to prepare, what it means to wait.

Come, Lord Jesus!

God of My Heart

"Faithful friends are beyond price; no amount can balance their worth" (Sirach 6:15).

God of Friends,

Friends are the greatest. A true friend is one of the most cherished possessions I could ever wish to have. My friends have stood by me through a lot and they have always been there for me.

Help me to remember this, God, when material things seem to matter more than they should, such as when I am Christmas shopping. While gifts are important and fun to get and give, I know that spending time with my friends and family is even more important than any gift. People are the real treasures, not material goods, although advertisers would have us believe otherwise. When I get caught up in material things, help me to remember the value of my family and friends and what a precious gift our time together is.

Today I will treat every friend, every family member, as the valuable gifts that they are in my life.

Julie Brown

Themes: friends, family,
        material goods, gifts

"Now faith is the assurance of things hoped for, the conviction of things not seen" (Hebrews 11:1).

God of Faith,

There are many times that I find myself being a nonbeliever. I doubt things that cannot be proven or seen. Sometimes I don't understand your ways, and that makes me doubt. Like now, during Advent, I wonder why you came as a baby and why you chose the conditions you did.

What is it you are saying to me during this time of preparation for Christmas? Help my faith in you to grow, no matter how many questions or doubts I have. Help me to understand that faith is a gift, and I don't need to understand everything. Help me to believe what is seen and unseen and to trust in your ways.

Today I will have faith in myself, in you and in others around me.

Teresa Harvat

Themes: doubt, faith

11

God of My Heart

"So have no fear of them; for nothing is covered up that will not be uncovered, and nothing secret that will not become known" (Matthew 10:26).

God of Courage,

I am faced with many challenging decisions. Many of them are yet unclear. I am afraid that I might make the wrong choices. I must look clearly at all the options even though the answers are not revealed to me. Continuing to work hard and not putting things off seems like the best solution to this difficult task. Not thinking negative thoughts and keeping a positive perspective on things will lead to a happier and more fulfilled life.

In this Advent time, I ask you, God, to grant me wisdom and show me the way. I need encouragement to discipline myself not to put things off.

Today I will not procrastinate.

Joel Schaaf

Themes: decisions, positive attitude, procrastination

"This people honors me with their lips, but their hearts are far from me" (Matthew 15:8).

God of My Life,

We often say that we are close and have a good relationship with you, but how many of us are telling the truth? Sometimes it's just easier to say the words and think that we are close and forget that we have to work at building a friendship with you.

I want to *be* close to you, not just *say* that I am, especially in this time of preparing for Christmas. Please give me the grace to hold you close in my heart and show you that I mean what I say through my actions.

Today when I pray, I will *think about* and *mean*, rather than just *say*, the words.

Matt Voss

Themes: prayer, truth,
intimacy with God

God of My Heart

"O Lord, do not rebuke me in your anger, or discipline me in your wrath. Be gracious to me, O Lord, for I am languishing" (Psalm 6:1-2a).

God of All Understanding,

There are many times in my life when the stress of school, family and work really gets me down. I feel trapped, and I just want to get into bed and hide from reality. These times of stress and chaos are when I need your love and support the most. Help me remember that. Just knowing that you won't leave me when I need you or that you won't get mad at me because I'm worried and upset makes those hard times a little easier.

During this time of Advent when I get stressed out over all the little, unimportant things that go wrong or all the many tasks I have to do, help me to ask for your help in doing them and then to calm down, relax and see the big picture.

Today I will make an effort to relax. When I feel I'm getting stressed I will ask for your help.

Heidi Waldschmidt

Themes: hard times, stress

14

"So whenever you give alms, do not sound a trumpet before you, as the hypocrites do in the synagogues and in the streets, so that they may be praised by others. Truly I tell you, they have received their reward. But when you give alms, do not let your left hand know what your right hand is doing so that your alms may be done in secret; and your Father who sees in secret will reward you" (Matthew 6:2-4).

All-Giving God,

Helping needy people in today's world does make a person look good. It says that we *are* trying. But many of us don't see the true "magic" in helping others. It is not the recognition or the rewards but the feeling inside, the deep satisfaction of giving of oneself that transforms us. It is true that we end up receiving more than we give.

This day, during this Advent season, was given to me by you, God, so let me make the most of it. When others need help or are having trouble, guide me to give a hand when it's needed and not make a big deal of it. When I help a classmate with their homework or give money to a homeless person on the street, I know that being able to help is reward enough. Thank you for the opportunity to give to others and for the experience of the true joy of giving that comes from it.

Today when I give to others, whether it be my money or my time, I will leave it at that and not seek thanks or recognition.

Jodi Boyd

Themes: selflessness, giving

God of My Heart

"Whoever loves discipline loves knowledge, but those who hate to be rebuked are stupid" *(Proverbs 12:1).*

Challenging God,

I cannot take criticism. I rebel against it, even if I know it may be more helpful to change. I am blind sometimes and cannot see that when I don't correct my mistakes I am only harming myself. Constructive criticism is a positive step toward improvement whether that be in character or physical appearance.

I know that others are only trying to help me become a better person when they give me constructive criticism. Show me that it's not so awful to admit I may be less than perfect, maybe even wrong. I will make mistakes, but I will strive to be wise enough to listen to others and open my eyes wide enough to examine and correct my faults.

Especially during this time of Advent, God, I will work at accepting constructive criticism in the spirit that it's given.

Shelley Buettner

Themes: criticism, mistakes, growth

"The Lord is my light and my salvation; whom shall I fear?"
(Psalm 27:1a).

God of Good Choices,

In my life there are many different twists and turns. Sometimes I get so mixed up that I don't know where to go. I am afraid of so many social pressures: drinking, drugs, sex and others.

God, please lead me to your light and take away my unreasonable fears. You and I can get through tough situations together. During this Advent season let me take a positive step out into life and not fear what may come of it. Grant me strength and wisdom to understand that I have nothing to fear when I confide in you and follow your will. Please work through me to give others the strength they need not to fear what they do not know.

Today I will do what I know is right no matter what my peers may think.

Danielle Cooper

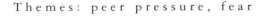

Themes: peer pressure, fear

God of My Heart

"You love all words that devour, O deceitful tongue" (Psalm 52:4).

Word of God,

There are many things about myself that I would like to change. The one that I most often ignore is gossiping. I need to consider students' and teachers' feelings when I say things about them. I need to learn what thoughts to keep to myself so that my words won't hurt someone else and cause them pain.

I ask you, God, to be in my thoughts as I talk. Be with me this Advent and remind me, as I speak, that I have the power to hurt other's feelings or to help them feel better about themselves.

Today I am going to make someone's day happier by choosing my words carefully.

Matt Cosson

Themes: gossip, change, speech

"For wisdom is a kindly spirit, but will not free blasphemers from the guilt of their words; because God is witness of their inmost feelings, and a true observer of their hearts, and a hearer of their tongues" (Wisdom 1:6).

All-Knowing God,

We arc the only creatures to whom you granted wisdom, the wisdom to know right from wrong, the wisdom to better our lives. But sometimes I think I'm smarter than you. I think I can deceive you. When others think I'm helping the situation, sometimes I'm really hurting it. Sometimes when people think that I'm doing my homework, I'm actually copying it from a friend. Help me to use your gift of wisdom in a positive way and to be honest with myself as well as others. I know that is a big part of being a wise person.

Thank you for the gift of wisdom. When I think about it, I know that even though I can fool my family and friends, I can't deceive you because you see everything. You even know what I am thinking.

On this day in Advent, I will use my gift of wisdom and do the best that I can do in all my studies.

Jason Grennan

Themes: wisdom, honesty, studies

God of My Heart

"When they saw that the star had stopped, they were over-whelmed with joy" (Matthew 2:10).

God of Our Growing Years,

Joy is a wonderful emotion to feel. Others can often see it on our faces.

I used to watch a young neighbor girl play in her yard. There was a treehouse that her older brother and his friends occupied. She wasn't allowed in the treehouse because she was too small. One summer there was a leaf hanging unusually low, and many times, when she thought no one was watching, she would go out and stretch up to touch it. She was never quite tall enough until one day toward the end of the summer she stood on her tiptoes and she finally did it. She touched the leaf! She didn't pick it, just gently touched it. I witnessed the joy rise in her face. She told no one. All she needed was to know that she could reach that leaf. She had grown! She knew it wouldn't be too long before she would be up in that treehouse. She could taste the possibility! But for now it was enough just to experience her joy.

Help me, God, to grow in the same simple way as that little girl this Advent. Thank you for the seemingly unimportant times of growth—the small joys—that you allow us to experience and enjoy.

Today I will add joy to someone's hectic life.

Julie Hoffman

Themes: joy, growth, goals

20

"Keep alert, stand firm in your faith, be courageous, be strong. Let all that you do be done in love" (1 Corinthians 16:13-14).

God of Love,

If only our attitude toward life was as simple as these verses that sum up all of life. We need to be alert in waiting for Jesus to come again. When trials and tribulations that we just can't understand come our way, we have the opportunity to stand firm in our faith. Having a brave and strong faith will get us through the challenges of life. Most importantly, we must treat all persons, guard all actions and do all our work *in love.* It all seems very logical and simple, but it is hard to do.

Please God, help me remember and refer back to these few, powerful words as I go about my day. When things are rushed and time is short, help me to do all my work in love. When people say words that hurt me, help me to be brave and strong and work my way through the hurt. And last of all, when I doubt your plans and your love for me, help me to stand firm in the struggle and know my faith in you will not fail me.

Today I will offer all my work and study as a gift of love in preparation for Christmas.

Lynn Smith

Themes: strength, love

21

Christmas

The Season of Christmas

Christmas! Incarnation! God with us! Our Christmas prayers center on gifts—the gift of Jesus, the gift of family, the gift of presence, the gift of joy. Christmas is indeed a miracle! We view the Christmas miracle from several different angles in the scriptural reflections that follow.

"Then he sent them to Bethlehem, saying, 'Go and search dili-gently for the child; and when you have found him, bring me word so that I may also go and pay him homage'" (Matthew 2:8).

God of Christmastime,

Every year we put up our tree and buy presents, but we know from experience this isn't where we find Jesus. It's not easy to find him, especially in today's world. The search is harder than ever. The birth of Jesus isn't just something that happened a long time ago, it happens everyday. We can see the miracle of Christ's birth in the miracles around us. We only need to search a little.

This holiday season I am going to seek out Jesus in the people around me. It is so obvious if I only look and really see. Please God, let me see through your eyes for at least a few minutes. I won't let it stop there, I will also worship Christ in the way I act toward others.

Today, I will be aware of the miracles happening all around me during this Christmas season.

Lisa Fitzpatrick

Themes: miracles, Jesus, Epiphany

God of My Heart

"The fruit of the Spirit is love, joy, peace, patience, kindness, generosity, faithfulness, gentleness and self-control" *(Galatians 5:22-23a).*

Joy-Giving God,

Today, I feel so kind; I delivered Christmas baskets. We spent time working on each family's boxes and their gifts. It was truly proof to me that when we let you into our lives and let you be a part of what we do, you bless us with wonder and joy. The good feeling that I experienced when doing this service for my Christmas family is amazing! I only hope that all of us can experience a similar joy by lending a hand in such a project this Christmas season.

God, I pray that you will help all those who don't have even what we consider necessities, so that they may have a comfortable, joy-touched Christmas. I also pray that we who help in these projects will never forget the experience and will continue to share the gifts that we've been given.

Today, I will make it a point to share in a most generous way with someone in need.

Shelly Byrne

Themes: joy, service, sharing, poverty

"Bless the Lord, O my soul. O Lord my God, you are very great. You are clothed with honor and majesty..." (Psalm 104:1a).

Awesome God,

You are the greatest! I love you! You have given me the best thing anyone could have, and that is life! That is the greatest gift possible. You came as a child to share in our life, our strengths and our weaknesses.

I thank you very much for my life. In return, I will love you and praise you all the days of my life. Thank you for your Christmas gift of yourself, for becoming one of us.

Today I am going to praise you, God, for giving me life. I am going to go out and have fun during this Christmas vacation.

Don Steffes

Themes: praise, thanks, life, fun

"Children, obey your parents in everything, for this is your acceptable duty in the Lord" (Colossians 3:20).

God of Love,

I want to thank you for my mom and dad. Even though we do have arguments and sometimes things get real tough, help me to understand them. Help them to understand me.

Please help me to realize that they love me and that they are trying, just like I am. I really like being close to them. They are such an important part of my life. It is because of them that I am who I am.

Today I will tell my parents that I love them and that I appreciate all they do for me.

Terra Kruse

Themes: parents, Holy Family, family

"He said, 'I am the voice of one crying out in the wilderness.
"Make straight the way of the Lord,"' as the prophet Isaiah
said" (John 1:23).

God of Inner Peace,

When John the Baptizer said these words in the desert, you were
working through him. John spent his life working to spread your
word. You asked him to baptize you even as he protested, "I am
not worthy to untie the thong of your sandal."

Sometimes I feel that you, God, are trying to work through me
too, but I sometimes shut you out and won't allow it. I do want
to do what is right, but I easily give in to pressures.

God, help me to help you. When you are working through me,
help me be aware of it, and help me to listen to my desire to do
what is right. What is it that you have in mind for my life, God?

Today I will be open to all the possibilities you have in store for
me.

Brian Harvat

Themes: vocation, Baptism of Our Lord

God of My Heart

"For where two or three are gathered in my name, I am there among them" (Matthew 18:20).

God of All,

It is important for me to remember that no matter what I do and no matter where I go, you will always be with me. You are constantly by my side, guiding me and helping me. You are in everyone around me. If I look, I can see you in other people.

God, I ask you to fill my day with experiences of you. Help me to see you in the actions and words of my friends, my family and all other people.

Today I will enjoy and appreciate the goodness of people around me.

Michelle Perlinger

Themes: guidance, God's presence, intimacy with God

The Season of Lent

The forty days of Lent offer a "time out" for giving, prayer, penance and fasting as we journey towards Easter. Well aware of the implication of sin in our lives, we can both give and receive forgiveness, which is an essential part of the Lenten journey.

In the following reflections, the need for prayer and a relationship with God is also evident. Easter only happens when we are willing to struggle through what we perceive to be darkness. We do the best we can with what we have and who we are at each particular moment in time. When Jesus "Easters" in us, we step into new light!

God of My Heart

"Whoever gives to the poor will lack nothing, but one who turns a blind eye will get many a curse" (Proverbs 28:27).

God of the Poor,

I need to realize that there are a lot of people who are less fortunate than I am. I could help by giving just a little more when the collection basket comes around in church every week. I could be more eager in volunteering for service that helps those in need. I could also use a push in the area of generosity. Possessions are so important to me.

Help me God, to go out of my way to be more giving, not only of material things but non-material things, like my time and talents.

Today I will look around and notice people's needs. I will do whatever I can to help.

Ann Larsen

Themes: giving, material goods, poverty, sharing

"Weeping may linger for the night, but joy comes with the morning" (Psalm 30:5b).

Compassionate God,

So many times I worry myself to tears. I overexaggerate or become paranoid about things over which I have no control. So many times I cry myself to sleep at night wondering if my pain will ever cease. Why must I be the one who struggles so hard to let go of love?

Help me, God, to realize that tomorrow is a new day and that my pain of worry and lost love will not last forever. Help me to let go of him and let me see some good that might come of this hurt. With you by my side I will have the courage to face my pain and let go of a love grown cold.

Today I will turn my pain over to you. I will let go of it. Is that perhaps one of the lessons of Lent?

Michelle Hinze

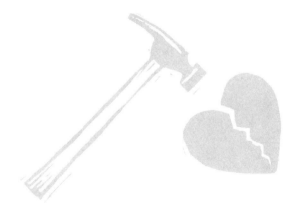

Themes: worries, pain, lost love

God of My Heart

"I become afraid of all my suffering, for I know you will not hold me innocent. I shall be condemned; why then do I labor in vain?" (Job 9:28-29).

Helping God,

In my life everything always seems to go wrong all at once. I am left alone, a disaster occurs, and I have to clean it all up. Why me? It takes all of my strength.

God, please help me to find time to get everything done, to weather this present disaster as well as the next one, and catch up on my sleep too. Give me what I need to make it through all of the bad times that come into my life, especially when they seem to happen all at once and I feel overwhelmed.

Today I will work through one problem at a time, knowing you are by my side.

Craig Branch

Themes: disaster, strength

"He said to them, 'Where is your faith?'" (Luke 8:25a).

Jesus,

You always know the right questions to ask. Indeed, where *is* my faith sometimes? More often than not, I am not sure where it is. When you took my grandfather from me, my first instinct was anger: "Why, God? What good is faith when things like this happen anyway?" I knew in my head that Grandpa would be happier in heaven than he was here, but it still hurt. I have faith that he is with Grandma now and as my ten year old sister put it, "eating steak and dancing."

Eternally present God, give me the depth of character I need to keep the faith in times when it is so tough. Allow me to be strong so that I can tolerate the times of pain and crisis. Help me never to forget that I am the one who "keeps the faith." It is a gift from you, but still my responsibility is to keep it alive.

Today I place my trust in you, God. Whether it's a good day or a bad one, I will remember that you are here for me. I will act in faith.

Mike Ruhlman

Themes: faith, trust, grief, death

33

God of My Heart

"Have mercy on me, O God, according to your steadfast love; according to your abundant mercy blot out my transgressions. Wash me thoroughly from my iniquity, and cleanse me from my sin" (Psalm 51:1-2).

Forgiving One,

You know that I have fallen away from you and your Church. Some days I barely even speak to you. When I use my tongue, it is to lash out at others, and then I feel justified.

God, I know I have many faults. I'm counting on your forgiveness. Help me to grow in the awareness of who you are in my life and how much you continue to love me. Stay with me even when I act like I want you to leave me alone.

Today I will watch my tongue and my temper. I will think about your steadfast love.

Lindsay Bryant

Themes: forgiveness, love, speech

34

"Teach me, and I will be silent; make me understand how I have gone wrong" (Job 6:24).

God of My Busy Days,

There are days when I am too busy with school work or my social life to see what I do wrong. I just do what I feel like and don't think about the consequences. I ignore my faults and go on with my life. When someone tries to talk to me about my faults, I look at it as jealousy or mean-spirited criticism.

God, during these busy days help me to be open-minded and see my faults so I don't continue to hurt the ones I love. Teach me through my friend's words that I do have faults, that having those faults is okay, and that I can work to correct them.

Today I will listen to others carefully and follow their good advice. I will be open to constructive criticism.

David Casillas

Themes: listening, criticism

God of My Heart

"Their iniquities are not hidden from him, and all their sins are before the Lord" (Sirach 17:20).

All-Knowing God,

Every day we sin and see others around us sin. Most of the time we choose to do wrong when we could choose to do right. Why is that, God? We ask for forgiveness and then we turn right around and deliberately repeat the wrongdoing.

Help us God, to learn from our wrong choices and help us to do what's right, even if we would rather do the thing that looks more appealing at the moment.

Today I will be conscious of the decisions I make. I will weigh the pros and cons before making a choice.

Trina Casillas

Themes: sin, decisions

36

"'Our law does not judge people without first giving them a hearing to find out what they are doing, does it?'" (John 7:51).

God of Equality,

Sometimes people unfairly judge others. A lot of times people are assumed to be someone or something they are not. We don't even give them the benefit of the doubt.

Please give me the grace, God, to look past my first impressions of people. Allow me to look inside at their hearts. Help me to know them. With you by my side, I know I can meet this challenge.

Today I will give people the benefit of the doubt.

Liz Clonch

Themes: fairness, judging

God of My Heart

"He called upon the Most High, the Mighty One, when ene-
mies pressed him on every side, and the great Lord answered
him with hailstones of mighty power" (Sirach 46:5).

God of Strength,

Every day we confront the enemies *darkness* and *fear*. Through you
we can become strong. We can dispel this darkness. We can overcome the fear.

But sometimes it seems impossible. We want to give in to fear and
darkness.

When we pick out people in the class to scapegoat, we let the
darkness take over. Because of our fear of peer pressure, we make
fun of them, hurt them and cause them to feel unwanted. Help us
realize the pain that we cause through our harsh, taunting words.
Help me to let my classmates know that what we do and say to
this person is wrong. We ask for forgiveness and for help overcom-
ing this darkness in our lives.

Today I will stand up for and defend the class scapegoats. Let me
be empathetic and treat them with respect.

Danielle Cooper

Themes: darkness, empathy, peer pressure

"Insults have broken my heart, so that I am in despair. I looked for pity, but there was none; and for comforters, but I found none" (Psalm 69:20).

Loving God,

Sometimes people can be so cruel and hateful. A lot of people hurt one another intentionally through insults and wrong judgements. Sometimes my heart just breaks because of the hurtful words and actions I see and hear, and I get weary trying to right the wrongs around me. I feel nobody notices or cares and it's just easier to let it all go, to ignore it.

Help us all continue to be strong enough to face the pain and sorrow in life and to right the wrongs when we can. Dry our tears and replace them with smiles and laughter. Help us to believe strongly in ourselves and in each other. Let us see that we all have a purpose in life, a mission to complete. Let us realize how precious life is and how blessed we are.

Today I will do all that I can to mend the broken hearts around me and to keep other hearts from breaking.

Lisa Fleck

Themes: hurts, purpose, empathy, peace

God of My Heart

"If you faint in the day of adversity, your strength being small.., does not he who keeps watch over your soul know it?" (Proverbs 24:10, 12b).

God of My Life,

When life is simple and things are going right, then being moral and treating everyone good is easy. When I am tested though, when stress seems to engulf me, I can forget the ideals and principles that I believe in so strongly. Then it's not easy at all!

God, give me the strength to remain constant through the difficult times so I can uphold my values. I wish to remain firmly set in my ideals, especially when it is "inconvenient" to follow through with them.

Today I will stand up for what I believe.

Libby Halley

Themes: trials, principles

"Happy are those who consider the poor, the Lord delivers them in the day of trouble" (Psalm 41:1).

God of the Oppressed,

Many times I look at the poor with great sympathy and sadness, yet I seldom do anything to help them. Someday I may be in their place, and if so, I will want more than sympathy, I will want a way out.

Help us to remember not to judge people by their finances. Help me to be generous in my volunteering as well as in my financial giving. Help me to always respect the poor, because I don't know what led to their poverty. I will do my best not to turn my back on them in their need. Help me to see what needs to be done and do it.

Today I promise to give generously to those in need.

Brian Harvat

Themes: respect, poverty, sharing
judging

God of My Heart

"So David prevailed over the Philistine with a sling and a stone, striking down the Philistine and killing him; there was no sword in David's hand" (1 Samuel 17:50).

God of Strength,

I pray to you for the strength and courage of David as I go into the battlefield of today's world. I pray to have faith in myself and in the people around me.

Help me to do the right thing and to have the determination of David to overcome all odds. Help me to stand up for what is right and to defeat the evil in the world today, one small victory at a time.

Today my courage will help me to do the right thing. I will be strong and stand up for what is right.

J. Jason Seberger

Themes: strength, faith, courage

"And forgive us our debts, as we also have forgiven our debtors" (Matthew 6:12).

God of Love,

How many times have we heard the words *forgive and forget?* Thousands, I'm sure. But how many times have we actually acted upon those words? So many things are so easy to say, but so hard to do. This is one of the very hardest things for me. If we are to sincerely love everyone, we must forgive the wrongs done against us, as small or as great as they seem. Forgiveness is the first step to healing all broken relationships, the first step to true reconciliation with others and with our God.

Help me to forgive at least one person for something they did to me in the past. Help me recall the incident without bias, consider the circumstances regarding all involved, realize the wrong done, forgive the person and then finally forget the incident. When these steps are followed, true forgiveness will be given and I can forget the hurt. Through this process my relationship with the other person grows and I can be sure the gift of forgiveness has been given. God, give me the strength and courage it takes to be this kind of person, the kind who forgives and forgets in the truest sense.

Today I will work on forgiving and forgetting my hurts from the past.

Lynn Smith

Themes: forgiveness, hurts, Lord's Prayer

43

God of My Heart

"Jesus himself stood among them and said to them, 'Peace be with you.' He said to them, 'Why are you frightened, and why do doubts arise in your hearts?'" (Luke 24:36b, 38).

Jesus, Healer,

All those times in my life when I blamed you for the bad things that happened, I later regretted because good came of them. When hard times hit, I often find myself asking, "What good could possibly come of this? How can I or my family benefit from such a tragedy?"

We experienced a tragic death; it brought us closer. We experienced a painful divorce; it made us see how lucky we've been with successful marriages. We went through the pain and unpredictableness of someone's cancer; it made us stronger to witness his strength pull him through. Now when dark times come around, I begin to search for the rainbows that appear at the end of every storm.

Today I will share this truth with someone who needs to hear it.

Carrie Fleck

Themes: tragedy, growth, perseverance

44

"I hereby command you: Be strong and courageous; do not be frightened or dismayed, for the Lord your God is with you wherever you go" (Joshua 1:9).

God of My Life,

I know that my problems are very small compared to some of the things facing the world today. When I start to complain and pout, I think about my friend who's facing the biggest challenge of his life, *death*. That gives me the strength to lift my head and deal with my life.

Please give me the strength I need to press on when things get tough. Help me to realize that things could be much worse. Help me never to give up when I face life's hard and trying struggles. I place my trust in you.

Today I will not complain about my troubles, instead I will count the blessings in my life.

Jason Cooper

Themes: complaining, blessings, perseverance

God of My Heart

"For evils have encompassed me without number, my iniquities have overtaken me, until I cannot see; they are more than the hairs of my head, and my heart fails me. Be pleased, O Lord, to deliver me; O Lord, make haste to help me" (Psalm 40:12-13).

God of My Journey,

There are times in my life when my problems outweigh my joys and it's hard to see the good and glorious. I know that when things get me down and I can't see the road ahead, it's hard to keep going, to keep up my courage for facing daily life.

Unfortunately, these troubled times are usually the only times I notice your presence. I suddenly remember that you are around when I have to take a test or when I'm in the midst of a fight with a friend. During the good times you rarely hear from me.

I'm going to change that. I will start by remembering and reliving the "Palm Sunday experiences" I've already had along my journey. Those were the glorious times, times when all was going the way I had hoped and dreamed. You were with me on those roads too.

Today I will take time to thank you, God, for being here with me in the good times as well as the bad.

Heidi Waldschmidt

Themes: Palm Sunday, thanks, good times, troubles

"In the morning, while it was still very dark, he got up and went out to a deserted place, and there he prayed" (Mark 1:35).

God of My Busy Days,

Most of the times when I pray, I pray as part of a community. I need to learn to go off alone and pray one-on-one with you. I know that if I would do this, you and I would become much closer. When I get caught up in the hassles of life, I know that prayer can radically slow down the pace. Ash Wednesday could be considered a wake-up call for my prayer life.

When my day seems hectic and full of problems, I need to take time out to pray for a calm spirit. Lent is a perfect time for me to do this. I know I can do this on my own or with a community of friends. It seems so simple but I make it so complicated. No matter how I pray, I know you'll be there to listen and slow me down when I need that extra peace.

Today, Ash Wednesday, I will make time to pray some private prayer.

Jodi Boyd

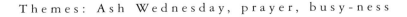

Themes: Ash Wednesday, prayer, busy-ness

God of My Heart

"And Jesus said to them, 'Follow me and I will make you fish for people'" (Mark 1:17).

Lord Jesus,

I truly believe that if we follow you, our lives will be so much more meaningful.

I could never imagine a life without faith in you. I know, however, that not everyone in this world believes in you. I follow you because I have been taught by those whom I admire. Help me to learn to follow you out of the convictions of my heart; to go to church and receive communion not because I'm expected to, but because I want to. I find it easy to call on you, but still I often find myself choosing poorly and doing the wrong thing in spite of my better judgement. Thank heavens I know I can always come to you for forgiveness.

Help me to follow my convictions more often.

Today I will do or say something in class or conversation out of conviction, not just because it is expected of me.

Shelly Byrne

Themes: Holy Thursday, convictions

48

"...Then he bowed his head and gave up his spirit" (John 19:30b).

All-Knowing God,

Jesus was a good friend to many people. I know how it hurts when a good friend dies or goes away. It's a loss that takes a long time to work through. Those who knew and loved Jesus must have had similar feelings.

Lord, help me to appreciate the memories I have of those who are no longer in my life. Help me realize what great gifts they added to my life. I treasure the memories of those who have left me and those who have died.

Today I will appreciate the friends that I have. I will be thankful for the time I have with them.

Terra Kruse

Themes: Good Friday, appreciation, friends, death

49

Easter

The Season of Easter

Alleluia! Resurrection! In the Church year we are now into the "peak season" of Christian living. We are invited to put the tough times behind us, at least for a while, and bask in the "aha!" moments of Jesus' resurrection. The reflections that follow explore our various perspectives in understanding the reality of the risen Christ in our lives.

"I am grateful to Christ Jesus our Lord, who has strengthened me, because he judged me faithful and appointed me to his service" (1 Timothy 1:12).

God of Laughter,

I need your strength. Right now I'm stressed; I'm pulled in too many different directions. My boss wants me to work, my coach wants me to practice, I need to do homework and yet I want to be with my friends. I feel so weak, like putty pulled and stretched. Some days I wake up and wonder, is this all there is to life?

People tell me that you, God, are watching over me all the time. I believe that. Take stress from me today and help me begin with a fresh new view, one that is peace filled and stress free. Help me realize that life is beautiful and needs to be fun. There *is* resurrection.

Today I will take a time-out, if only for ten minutes, and do something fun: look through some old pictures, do something silly—anything to bring back some good memories.

Jason Grennan

Themes: stress, fun

God of My Heart

"Now faith is the assurance of things hoped for, the conviction of things not seen" (Hebrews 11:1).

God of Trust,

Why do we doubt what we cannot see? Why must we question what we cannot easily prove? Is it our nature to be like Thomas? It's so hard not to do this. Why must something be real only when one or more of our senses says it is? When we get discouraged and lose hope, it is even harder to believe and keep believing.

God, help us put aside the human part of us that makes us doubt what we cannot prove. Make us realize that there is more to reality than just the tangible here and now. Help us to keep faith. Let us see Christ in those around us—and may that be our proof of your reality.

Today I will take note of all the things I believe in and realize that absolute knowledge is very rare.

Kathryn Siebert

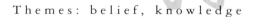

Themes: belief, knowledge

"No one has greater love than this, to lay down one's life for one's friends. You are my friends if you do what I command you. I do not call you servants any longer, because the servant does not know what the master is doing; but I have called you friends because I have made known to you everything that I have heard from my Father" (John 15:13-15).

God of Love,

There are so many people that come and go in our lives. Most are just acquaintances, but some become more than that; they become friends. Our friends are so important to us because they help mold us, they become a part of us, helping create our personalities. No person could survive—or even be *expected* to survive—without a friend.

And yet, when it seems there's no one there, I believe there will always be one friend we can count on—it's you, God, who will never fail us. No matter how many times we may fail, you love us unconditionally. Your death and resurrection give us this hope.

And you, God, are like the rest of us—or I should say, we're like you. All of your creation reveals who you are, just as our friends reveal who we are.

Today I'll be especially grateful to my friends and go out of my way to do a favor for them.

Trina Casillas

Theme: friends

God of My Heart

"Peace I leave with you; my peace I give to you. I do not give to you as the world gives. Do not let your hearts be troubled, and do not let them be afraid" (John 14:27).

Comforter God,

You give us people to share with to ease our minds. You tell us not to worry, because you will always be here for us. You tell us not to be afraid because you have gone before us. You are risen from the dead. "Been there, done that."

Even so, it is hard for me to let go and trust you. Today I'm worried and upset. For instance, if I get one more ounce of homework, I feel I will break. Will tomorrow ever get here?

God, I pray that I will let you take my worries about school and home away from me. Help me see that you won't give me any more than I can handle. I know I can't handle this alone. Help me realize that I don't have to. Please help bring peace to my life.

Today I will concentrate on one project at a time. I know that together you and I can handle anything.

Lisa Fitzpatrick

Themes: trust, worries, studies

"And not only that, but we also boast in our sufferings, knowing that suffering produces endurance, and endurance produces character, and character produces hope..." (Romans 5:3-4).

God of My Struggle,

Some days it feels like the whole world is out to get me and everything in my life is going wrong. When I'm having a bad day, it's so hard to see the good things that are continually taking place. The hope of resurrection seems unreal.

God, when things don't go my way, I am going to remember that there are always wonderful things happening in my life, even if they are difficult to see. Help me to grow stronger because of the troubles that I endure. Help me to realize that through my endurance, I will create a chain reaction as I grow closer to you.

Today I will look at my troubles in a new light—I will think about how they have made me a stronger person.

Jenny Love

Themes: troubles, strength

God of My Heart

"But for your holy ones there was very great light" (*Wisdom 18:1a*).

God of Miracles,

I believe you are light. Resurrection is everywhere! Sometimes, though, we are blind to your light, and things get in the way of our seeing your light. You put your light right here under our noses, and we still often miss it. We see it when children sing and people laugh in wholesome ways. We see it when elderly people who have difficulty walking get out on the dance floor and spin and twirl. We also experience your light when we are not paying attention and accidentally run a stop sign and then, after realizing it, breathe a sigh of relief that no one was coming the other way. When the underdog wins the game, your light shines again.

Thanks for your many lights, God. Help us all to be more aware and appreciative of them.

Today I will look for your miracles and appreciate your brilliant light that is so obvious in the happenings around me.

Julie Hoffman

Themes: light, miracles

"The hope of the righteous ends in gladness, but the expectation of the wicked comes to nothing" (Proverbs 10:28).

God of Challenge,

Looking forward is what keeps me going; I know that things will get better. Right now, though, life is rough, and there are many stressful activities pulling at my limited time. There is a lot of uncertainty in my life.

Give me hope, God, that I may know there is more to life than this hole that I have dug my way into. Help me realize that resurrection is a reality. Guide me to make the best decisions I can, so I may live a good and full life—and be happy singing your praises.

Today I will not complain about the burdens I have; I will view them as challenges I have been asked to meet.

Mike Ruhlman

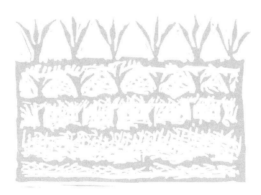

Themes: hope, challenge, perseverance

God of My Heart

"Do not boast about tomorrow, for you do not know what a day may bring. Let another praise you, and not your own mouth—a stranger, and not your own lips. A stone is heavy, and sand is weighty, but a fool's provocation is heavier than both" (Proverbs 27:1-3).

God of Humility,

Now and then I take too much pride in my actions and accomplishments. I then become boastful and speak out in an effort to gain attention and praise. I sometimes intentionally intimidate others so that I can succeed. In the ongoing struggle to make myself look and feel better, I often lift myself up by holding others down.

God, help me to stay humble and gracious at all times. With your aid, God, I believe that I can take praise in an appropriate manner while helping those around me to improve themselves as well. I think that's part of your Easter message.

Today I will not let glory and pride weaken my accomplishments by weakening my character.

Mike Zalewski

Themes: pride, character

"From the fruit of the mouth one is filled with good things, and manual labor has its reward" (Proverbs 12:14).

God of Gifts,

At times I work really hard, yet it seems that no one notices. I just want my effort to be recognized. I need to understand that simply doing my best makes me a better, stronger person, whether or not Mom and Dad, my coach or a teacher notices.

Please, God, give me the knowledge to realize my potential and the strength to live up to my potential. Let me develop my talents through hard work, so I can achieve what I set forth to obtain. Let Easter be a reality in my life. Show me how to help those who are struggling as I am. When I have reached my goals, give me the vision to see that you gave me the potential to succeed. Help me never to take my gifts for granted.

Today I will work toward my goal and help others who are striving to achieve their goals as well.

Brian Boerner

Themes: talents, recognition

God of My Heart

*"Why are you cast down, O my soul, and why are you disqui-
eted within me? Hope in God; for I shall again praise him,
my help and my God" (Psalm 42:11).*

God of Guidance,

When things don't go my way in life, I know you will give me the
strength to get past them. But sometimes I lose faith; I doubt that
you even care about me.

When it seems like no one is on my side and that everyone is
against me, please help me to be strong, to experience the joy of
resurrection. Let me realize that I'm not alone, and that you are
truly here for me, to lead me and to support me.

Today I will strive to have a positive outlook on all that happens
and trust in what you say.

Letitia Halverson

Themes: faith, support, God's presence

60

"A cheerful heart is a good medicine, but a downcast spirit dries up the bones" (Proverbs 17:22).

Life-Giving God,

Sometimes it is so hard for me to be cheerful. The world seems like such a mess. I look around and see crime and violence and it depresses me. But then there are times I can look at the world in the opposite way and see that is not such a terrible place after all. Maybe it all has something to do with death and resurrection.

Help me, God, to keep a positive outlook on life, to be kind to others and to learn from my mistakes. Even though life can be rough, violent and full of crime, I want to stay optimistic; I want to focus on the resurrection. I know that with your help I can.

Today I will be a positive force in any group meeting or discussion.

Michelle Perlinger

Themes: violence, optimism

God of My Heart

"Take delight in the Lord, and he will give you the desires of your heart" (Psalm 37:4).

God of Life,

When I'm by myself and have nothing to do, I always look at the bad side of being alone. Why don't I have more to do that is fun and exciting? I don't want to do homework or help out at home—I want to have fun! Why can't I find something to do? Maybe there's a reason; maybe I need some time alone to think and to pray.

God, help me to remember that I can make every day fun some way or another even if I'm alone. It's all in my attitude. It's really you *and* me, so I am never alone.

Today I will examine my attitude and work on taking delight in the good that I see. This Easter season I will celebrate.

Beth Ranck

Themes: aloneness, attitude, fun, God's presence

"O magnify the Lord with me, and let us exalt his name together" (Psalm 34:3).

Jesus, My Brother,

Being Christian in today's world has its advantages. People look at Christians as good, honest people. When I wear my letter jacket people respect me and I have the opportunity to make a good impression, because by wearing it they know I go to a Christian school. That makes it important for me to live up to that good reputation, because whether I do something good or bad, it reflects on my church and on my school.

You set a fine example for us, Jesus. Help me to glorify your name by being a truly Christian young person who lives up to the good name of both my church and school communities. Help me to keep those names ones that we can be proud of.

Today I will live up to the name Christian and make the best moral decisions I can.

Matt Irish

Themes: example, self-respect

God of My Heart

"He heals the brokenhearted, and binds up their wounds"
(Psalm 147:3).

God of Victory,

There are times in my life when I feel conquered, physically and mentally. It is at those times that I am most vulnerable.

Then there are times, like in a basketball game, when we're down by ten points, and I feel like giving up, but an urge deep down inside comes to the surface and I have the strength to keep going. These are the times that I need you most, God. I know that your Spirit is that deep down urge that gives me a second wind. I know from experience that you'll always be there for me, and knowing this gives me a sense of security.

When I'm at my weakest, I will turn to you in prayer for the strength to keep going. Knowing what you have done for me in the past gives me courage to keep going now. You've never turned away from me, and I know you never will.

Today I will share with someone who seems down or depressed a story of one time when I got a "second wind"

Matt Irish

Themes: weakness, security, perseverance

64

"I will extol you, my God and King, and bless your name forever and ever" (Psalm 145:1).

God of My Questions and Answers,

So many times I forget that you are always right here for me to help me solve my problems. Day by day I go to others for help and figure they know how to help me. Oftentimes all they do is confuse me. Instead I could turn your way, and you will guide me. It is not that easy though. When I am at church I often just stare off in space, hoping it will be a short service; I always rejoice when I hear the last blessing. Why do I do this? I miss so many opportunities to grow closer to you.

God, help me see that the right way is you. You are the resurrection and the life. When I am at church, help me keep in mind the real reason I want to be there.

Today I will talk to you several times, knowing you are my best friend, wanting to deepen our friendship.

Beth Ranck

Themes: prayer, church, intimacy with
God

65

God of My Heart

"Praise the Lord! O give thanks to the Lord, for he is good; for his steadfast love endures forever. Who can utter the mighty doings of the Lord, or declare all his praise?" (Psalm 106:1-2).

God of My Joy,

You are such a merciful God. You show me your presence in people's lives. Your hand touches me and those around me. I see you repair old friendships and help make new ones. I see you in the lives of those in whom I confide, as well as in those who confide in me. Thank you for allowing me to enjoy and rejoice in their happiness.

Dear God, allow me to always see your signs and miracles, the joys of Easter, in those around me. Your miracles are such that we sometimes miss them. We have so many things in which to rejoice; the opportunity of today, our humanness, the weather and the country in which we live, just to name a few.

Today I will work at being more aware. I will praise you throughout the day for the miracles that take place daily in my life.

Matt Cosson

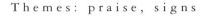

Themes: praise, signs

66

*"These all look to you to give them their food in due season;
when you give it to them, they gather it up; when you open
your hand, they are filled with good things" (Psalm 104:
27-28).*

Generous God,

Your generosity is so real in my life. Right now, I depend on you
for everything I need. Then sometimes I forget that you have given
it all to me, and I ignore your presence in my life. You give us
everything. If only we would realize your generosity and put to
better use the gifts you have given us: our lives, our opportunities,
our friends and even our enemies.

Help us, God, during this Eastertime, to be grateful and satisfied.
Let us see your hand in all things around us, even those we consider insignificant. Teach us to use and enjoy them as you
intended.

Today I will not be greedy. I will be thankful for all that I am and
all that you have given me.

Matt Voss

Themes: gifts, gratefulness

God of My Heart

"No one after lighting a lamp puts it under the bushel basket, but on the lampstand, and it gives light to all in the house. In the same way, let your light shine before others, so that they may see your good works and give glory to your Father in heaven" (Matthew 5:15-16).

Life-Giving God,

I know you have really made a difference in my life. I know how important you are to me, but I guess that is not enough.

I need to let others see the difference in me, so that they will want to believe in you too. I'm just beginning to understand that's what Pentecost is all about.

God, today let my words and actions reflect my belief in you. I know it won't be easy, but I can do it.

Lisa Fitzpatrick

Themes: Pentecost, example, witness

"But immediately Jesus spoke to them and said, 'Take heart, it is I; do not be afraid'" (Matthew 14:27).

God of New Beginnings,

Sometimes I'm really frightened of leaving my home and going away to school. I am going to miss my family desperately, and I'm not one who's crazy about change—this will be the biggest transition so far in my life.

Please help me to be more open to change and to realize that change is a form of growth. I know that you'll still be right with me and that my parents have raised me to be a responsible person with good judgment. Help me to trust myself as my family does.

Today I will write down three of my good qualities and rejoice in them.

Shelley Buettner

Themes: new beginnings, responsibility, change, growth

God of My Heart

"Jesus answered them, 'Truly I tell you, if you have faith and do not doubt, not only will you do what has been done to the fig tree, but even if you say to this mountain, "Be lifted up and thrown into the sea," it will be done. Whatever you ask for in prayer with faith, you will receive'" (Matthew 21:21-22).

God of All-Knowing,

The other night I sat in my bedroom, wondering about the mysteries of the universe and if there really was a God. The thought just jumped into my mind out of nowhere. I don't usually think about things like that; anyone who knows me will assure you of that. The very next day my father was reading to me from the Bible. The words that he read from that book rattled inside of me, and a feeling of joy rushed through me. I can't explain it, I just know how I felt.

God, please give me the strength, day in and day out, to keep the faith not only in my mind but also in my heart, so I can be aware of what your rising from the dead really means. Thank you for these kind of faith-filled moments. They keep me going.

Today I will be glad of my faith and say a prayer of thanks.

Mario Casillas

Themes: mystery, faith, scripture

70

"Come to me, all you that are weary and are carrying heavy burdens, and I will give you rest" (Matthew 11:28).

God of Life,

Why is it that we find it so hard to accept death? When a death occurs we tend to forget that our loved one is with you. Sometimes we lose our peace of mind and struggle for answers to a most complicated question.

We need to mourn, I know; that's part of being human and letting go. We also need to rejoice in the meaning of resurrection. Please help all of us who have suffered the loss of a loved one, so we may rediscover peace and joy in our lives.

Today I will help someone be at peace by comforting them and listening.

Shelly Byrne

Themes: death, resurrection

God of My Heart

"Then afterward I will pour out my spirit on all flesh; your sons and your daughters shall prophesy, your old men shall dream dreams, and your young men shall see visions" (Joel 2:28).

God of My Spirit,

As I read these words I am moved to give my total self in service to the less fortunate...even to help out my enemies. If every young person in the world could just share their vision, their positive spirit, then good things would happen. Until that day comes, I need to pray to do what is asked of me as an individual and as a young person. But sometimes I feel that if I continue to give myself to everyone else, I will have nothing left for me. I need to realize that giving myself to others makes more of me to give.

Help me to spread my good spirit to all, God, even those who ridicule and hurt me. I will open my heart and attempt to give back some of what you've given to me. If my parents seem like they are lacking open minds or my boss is nagging me, let me bounce back from that and give them what I have—"positive spirit."

Today I will realize the gift of my youth and share my good spirit.

Jodi Boyd

Themes: giving, positive attitude

"The Lord is my shepherd... He leads me in right paths for his name's sake" (Psalm 23:1a, 3b).

God of My Ups and Downs,

Some days I doubt your presence. I get side-tracked and head down the wrong road. I forget where I am going or why I am even going this way. I feel as though I am all alone and there is no one to whom I can turn. You seem very far away, especially when plans don't go my way.

Help me, God, to find you in my heart. Give me strength to walk the right road, for the right reasons, even though it may be long and rough. I believe in resurrection. Give me what it takes to help others travel along that same road.

Today I will encourage someone to do what is right, not because there's something in it for me, but just because it is the right thing to do.

David Casillas

Themes: aloneness, strength, God's presence

God of My Heart

"It is better to hear the rebuke of the wise than to hear the song of fools" (Ecclesiastes 7:5).

God of Lasting Friendship,

Oftentimes I feel like a failure. I look at other people and I think, "Why can't I be more like them?" Sometimes I wish I were more popular and more beautiful and more loved by everyone. I do know that I have close friends for whom I care deeply, and I know that I am lovable, but those negative feelings persist.

Help me to see that popularity is not an essential ingredient for happiness. Help me also to realize the value of my friends and not to take them for granted. Help me to be kind to people who have few friends or who are lonely, especially during this time of Easter.

Today I will enjoy my friends and let them know how much they mean to me.

Tina Cooper

Themes: popularity, friends

74

The Season of Ordinary Time

In the Church calendar, "Ordinary Time" covers the day to day happenings of the major part of the year. The Church views ordinary time as a time for continued growth. In the prayers that follow, we witness to simple, profound, everyday faith as we touch base with our God concerning the ordinary "stuff" of daily life.

God of My Heart

"I desire that you insist on these things so that those who have come to believe in God may be careful to devote themselves to good works; these things are excellent and profitable to everyone" (Titus 3:8b).

God of Goodness,

Who are today's heroes? Whom do we idolize? Violence and crime run rampant on today's streets. Some professional athletes whom we look up to are caught using drugs and provide terrible role-modeling. World leaders declare war and sentence people to death. We need some real heroes.

God, help me set an example for the people around me. Don't let me or my friends be influenced by the negative factors in today's world. Let my actions be a model for others, especially the younger people in my life. Help me to resist the glamour life—"live fast, die young." I want to be the best I can be; that means I want to include you in my life.

Today I will be conscious of the example I am setting for those who are younger than I am. I will make sure that what I do sets a good example.

Travis Mills

Themes: example, role models

76

"For we know, brothers and sisters beloved by God, that he has chosen you" (1 Thessalonians 1:4).

God of Love,

I understand I was chosen to be your own through the many blessings you've given me. My wonderful friends and family show your great love for me. But sometimes...well a lot of times...I don't feel worthy of your unconditional love or the love of my family and friends. Basically, I feel this way much of the time, because I do not love myself enough. This makes it difficult for me to love others, which in turn starts the cycle over. I feel unworthy again and again, and I find myself unable to love others again and again.

Help me, God, to realize that everything you made is good—and that includes me. I have proof right here in scripture.

Today I will think about at least three of my good qualities and be glad that I have them. I will remind myself that you made me...you made me *good!*

Shelley Buettner

Themes: blessings, self-love, unconditional love

God of My Heart

"In him we have redemption through his blood, the forgiveness of our trespasses, according to the riches of his grace" (Ephesians 1:7).

God of Forgiveness,

It is easy to forgive my friends, but those who are not my friends ...well, that's another story. When I think of how you forgive everyone, though, the thought makes me want to at least try to be more compassionate.

Please help me to pardon others, just as you have pardoned me so many times. I know I do not have to be everyone's best friend, but I do want to be able to get along with most everyone. That means I need to forgive more often. I am asking for your help with this, God.

Today I will forgive someone who has hurt me in some way.

Danni Szwanek

Theme: forgiveness

*"And do not grieve the Holy Spirit of God, with which
you were marked with a seal for the day of redemption"
(Ephesians 4:30).*

God of My Growing Years,

As we young adults move into an adult world, we gain more and
more freedom. With this freedom comes temptation, temptation
to turn away from God. Sin seems so much easier, but if we really
think about what we're doing and choose your way, then we can be
glad of our freedom and the wisdom of our choices. Thank you so
much for the gift of your inspiring Spirit in our lives, a Spirit that
can help us make good choices.

God, help us to think clearly about the roads we choose. Help us
to keep you in our hearts and minds as we make those choices.

Today I will think twice before I allow myself to compromise
my values. I will work at making the best choices I can, not the
easiest.

David Casillas

Themes: choices, freedom

God of My Heart

"Greet one another with a holy kiss. All the saints greet you. The grace of the Lord Jesus Christ, the love of God, and the communion of the Holy Spirit be with all of you"
(2 Corinthians 13:12-14).

God of Friendship,

Why do so many of the people around me wear frowns on their faces? It's hard to smile at others when no one smiles back. It doesn't hurt someone to share a smile or say hello. Why do so few do it?

Help me to persevere. Help me to show others your love within me in spite of those frowns around me. Let me keep in mind that where I seek good I will find it. Give me what it takes to see the bright side of things when others cannot.

Today I will keep a positive attitude toward whatever comes my way.

Kathryn Siebert

Theme: positive attitude, example

"And there are varieties of activities, but it is the same God who activates all of them in everyone. To each is given the manifestation of the Spirit for the common good"
(1 Corinthians 12:6-7).

God of Diversity,

I look at the people around me and become very jealous. I ask myself, "Why don't I know how to do what he does?" or "Why can't I look like she does?" I see so many special gifts from you in those around me, but I often can't find any special gifts inside myself.

I know my gifts from you are in there, I've just got to recognize them and use them. One of them might be the ability to help out a teacher, to make a friend feel better or maybe even just to laugh aloud.

Today I am going to dig down inside myself and find my special gifts from God.

Jenny Love

Themes: jealousy, gifts, attentiveness, self-love

God of My Heart

"However that may be, let each of you lead the life that the Lord has assigned, to which God called you" (1 Corinthians 7:17a).

God of Blessings,

It is often easier for me to give up and not use the talents you have given me than to continue to struggle to develop them.

Help me to recognize your gifts to me and not to give up on them. Please help me to bring out the best in myself even though it's sometimes difficult. I do want to lead the best Christian life that I can and follow in your footsteps.

Today I will look for the good in myself and others and build on it.

Rebekah Smith

Themes: talents, goodness, gifts, self-love

"It causes all, both small and great, both rich and poor, both free and slave, to be marked..." (Revelation 13:16).

God of Love,

Sometimes I just think, "If I could only be rich, I would have everything solved." It seems like money has power to make us happy; we crave it. I want to go to college, but only because I want a good job that will make me good money. I never stop to think if I could be happy being poor and just getting by. People say all you need to be happy are loving friends and family. I wish I could honestly believe that. I can see that money has too much power over me and pulls me away from you.

God, please help me to stop being so money hungry and to learn the value of love. Help me look at the happiness that loving and being loved can bring instead of how much happiness a $100.00 pair of jeans can bring.

Today I will think about my future in light of what will honestly bring me happiness.

Beth Ranck

Themes: love, money, material goods

God of My Heart

"Cast all your anxiety on him, because he cares for you"
(1 Peter 5:7).

God of Guidance,

I have never been able to just let you take care of things. I always have to be in control.

Help me to see how much simpler and richer life can be when you, not I, are the one in charge. Give me the courage to let you take control. Help me through my problems.

Today I will let go and let God be in charge.

Sally Oates

Themes: letting go, control

"If any of you is lacking in wisdom, ask God, who gives to all generously and ungrudgingly, and it will be given you" (James 1:5).

All-Knowing God,

Why do I feel so stupid sometimes? There are times when I try so hard to understand something, but it just won't "sink in."

Help me, God, to realize that wisdom is not grades or even intelligence. Wisdom is learning and understanding, and it comes from experience. Give me the insight to pray for wisdom, not necessarily for better grades. I pray, too, for the wisdom to see my problems and work through the ones I can.

Today I will empathize with someone when they're not feeling too intelligent. I will help them laugh and put into perspective what's really important.

Kathryn Siebert

Themes: grades, wisdom

God of My Heart

"Do not speak harshly to an older man, but speak to him as to a father, to younger men as brothers, to older women as mothers, to younger women as sisters—with absolute purity" (1 Timothy 5:1-2).

Ageless God,

When I was younger I used to go to my grandma's house. I would always ask myself, "Why am I here?" And I would answer myself by saying, "It's just part of being a grandson. It will make her happy." I felt like this for a long time, and I now know that's only half of the story. She is my elder and I do owe her my love and respect, but in the past I didn't always think of it in that way.

Now that I'm older, and hopefully wiser, I appreciate just being around Grandma. I appreciate the advice she gives me, the time she's spent with me. I truly love my grandmother for so many unspoken reasons. Thanks, God, for grandparents, they have taught us so many things.

Today I will remember my grandparents and call them just to say a quick "Hi," or I will drop them a note to let them know I'm thinking about them.

Albirio Madrid

Themes: grandparents, family

"Do all things without murmuring and arguing, so that you may be blameless and innocent, children of God without blemish in the midst of a crooked and perverse generation, in which you shine like stars in the world" (Philippians 2:14-15).

Dear God,

Whenever there is a chore for me to do around the house, I always end up whining about having to help out. My parents do so much for me; why do I whine and complain so much just because I'm asked to do my part? I find it really hard to volunteer to do a job without complaining about it. I don't understand myself.

Help me, God, to do my assigned tasks without one negative "peep." Let me go the extra mile.

Today I will take a look around the house and find something that needs to be done and do it without being told!

Ann Larsen

Themes: chores, whining, service, family

God of My Heart

"I will never leave you or forsake you" (Hebrews 13:5b).

God of the Here and Now,

Sometimes I get so wrapped up in what my future plans are that I don't stop to appreciate my life right now.

Help me to appreciate my family, my friends, my school, my teachers, my job and just life in general. Help me also to appreciate you, God; I so often forget. Help me realize that you are always in my life and in my heart.

Today I will literally take time to smell the flowers.

Jayna Schaaf

Themes: All Saints Day, appreciation

"Endure trials for the sake of discipline. God is treating you as children; for what child is there whom a parent does not discipline?" (Hebrews 12:7).

God of Peaceful Hearts,

You know when my life becomes hectic and overwhelming, when nothing goes the way I want. You know when I am struggling with a history assignment, a math test or a chemistry quiz. Often I lose my way, my sense of priorities.

A quick prayer can bring me back to you. When I pray, everything calms down and I realize I *can* handle anything if I just keep in touch with you. Let me make an effort to "roll with life's punches."

Today I will keep in touch with you all day long through short prayers. I will not let the pressures get the upper hand.

Danielle Cooper

Themes: pressures, prayer, God's presence

God of My Heart

"And you will know the truth, and the truth will make you free" (John 8:32).

All-Truthful God,

Many times I choose to keep opinions and feelings to myself. I think it's better that way, and sometimes it is, but sometimes it's not. I am aware that by keeping things to myself I can end up hurting others. In the long run, I may end up hurting myself too.

Please God, give me the courage to speak my mind more often and to become a more truthful person. Help me to realize that saying the truth when it is called for is always more beneficial than keeping it all inside.

Today I will make an effort to be more honest with others and myself.

Teresa Harvat

Themes: feelings, truth, speech

"No one has greater love than this, to lay down one's life for one's friends" (John 15:13).

God of Kindness,

The world sometimes makes it easier for me to buy friendship than to give myself. I need to be aware that every friend of mine is a gift from you and not something to be taken for granted.

Please help me to love and respect all of my friends. When the opportunity comes for me to show my love for them, help me to take advantage of that situation and do so. Help me to appreciate your unconditional love for me as the best gift of all.

Today I will be caring and kind, and thank you, God, for the gift of friends in my life.

Meaghan Thompson

Themes: friends, unconditional love, gifts

God of My Heart

"You know the commandments: ...Honor your father and mother" (Luke 18:20).

God of My Growing Years,

It seems that the older I get, the more independent I become. I'm beginning to be dependent upon myself rather than on my parents. The problem is, I'm beginning to totally avoid my parent's advice and ignore their wisdom. I realize that by doing this I am going through life the hard way. I also can see that my relationship with them is slowly falling apart. No matter what it looks like to them or to any other person, that is not what I want.

God, please be with me as I struggle to listen to my parents' words. I have much to learn from them as I go through life. I know with your help the learning process can be less painful.

Today I will work on being easier to live with, namely by listening to my parents' ideas about decisions I have yet to make.

Matt Cosson

Themes: parents, decisions, wisdom, growth

"For nothing is hidden that will not be disclosed, nor is anything secret that will not become known and come to light"
(Luke 8:17).

All-Knowing God,

When I try to hide things, I feel guilty. If I just face up to them, I know I will feel better about myself and be much happier. To keep things hidden away or covered up will get me nowhere, because even if I fool other people, I know you can still see it all. I know you see right through me. I want to be honest with myself and you.

Please help me, God. I don't want to keep things bottled up inside me. I am human and I make mistakes just like everyone else.

Today if I make a mistake, I will admit it and get on with my life.

Anne Marie Kuhlman

Themes: mistakes, honesty

God of My Heart

"At that time the disciples came to Jesus and asked, 'Who is the greatest in the kingdom of heaven?' He called a child, whom he put among them, and said, 'Truly I tell you, unless you change and become like children, you will never enter the kingdom of heaven'" (Matthew 18:1-3).

God of Attitudes,

I see you as the Most High. Your intention in creating us was to make us look good and feel great! You did a great thing by creating all the possibilities in our lives. You let us choose our own paths.

I choose to become like a child as you suggested, an innocent child. I want to be playful and loved, and someday enter your kingdom. Please help me to know what you mean by these words of yours, and help me to live them out in my life.

Today I will enjoy being a child of God by showing my joy when good things happen.

Chris Pierzina

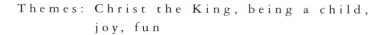

Themes: Christ the King, being a child, joy, fun

94

"But Jesus looked at them and said, 'For mortals it is impossible, but for God all things are possible'" (Matthew 19:26).

Creator God,

I think it's important for my family to get along, but when I try to bring my family closer together it seems impossible. No matter what I say, we end up fighting. Some of the fault lies in me, God, because I am selfish and I want everything to go my way. I know how much my parents care for me, and I want to change my stubborn ways.

Help me to take their thoughts and feelings into consideration when I feel a fight coming on. Help me to do my part to make my family one that respects each of its members, despite disagreements. When things seem impossible, give us the patience and concern to work things out.

Today I will not "add fuel to the fire" in any argument.

Monica Vega

Themes: arguments, family

God of My Heart

"Do not judge, so that you may not be judged" *(Matthew 7:1).*

God of Open Minds,

Many times I have not been patient with other people, but have tried to do things my own way without considering their thoughts or ideas.

Please give me the patience to listen to others and to see the good in their suggestions. Help me to not always insist that my way is the best way.

Today I will be patient, listen and seriously consider other's ideas.

Matt Perlinger

Themes: patience, listening

"Then Jesus told his disciples, 'If any want to become my followers, let them deny themselves and take up their cross and follow me'" (Matthew 16:24).

God of New Beginnings,

It's going to be hard leaving all my friends. It's going to be hard getting my life in order after I graduate. Finding the right college and the right job will be important. Maybe I should just stay here; maybe not.

Lord help me to accept that I'm growing up and that sooner or later I'm going to have to go out into the world and make it on my own. My friends are wonderful, but they can't live my life for me. I want to follow you, so please help me to do as you say and carry my own cross.

Today I'm going to decide to do what is right. and I will make that decision by myself.

Tara Larsen

Themes: graduation, growing up, decisions

God of My Heart

"...do not worry about how you are to speak or what you are to say..." (Matthew 10:19b).

Word of God,

Today I was thinking, when was the last time I called an old friend just to say "Hi" or wrote to my grandma to tell her I'm doing fine? We live in a fast-paced society. Information gets thrown around like a ball; we catch it if we can, but if we can't, we hope someone else will—and then we forget about it. True communication suffers.

I need to slow down, to take time to talk about what I am doing and how I am feeling, to quit worrying about the best way to go about it. I know there are several people who would enjoy talking with me or hearing from me.

Today I will take time to call an old friend and talk, or I will write a letter to someone and catch them up on all the news.

Julie Hoffman

Themes: communication, caring

"Then you call on the name of your god and I will call on the name of the Lord; the god who answers by fire is indeed God" (1 Kings 18:24a-b).

Powerful God,

Help me to remember that you are number one in my life. There is nothing as important to me as you. I'm sorry that sometimes I fail to remember this and I get caught up in the material world— in things like money, cars and human desires. Our world leads me to believe that I need to outdo others by possessing more and more things. My faith tells me that is not true.

Guide me and help me realize that you alone are my God. You alone are the one who is all important in my life; everything else is secondary. You are my Creator and Savior.

Today I resolve to remember that you, God, are the reason that I am here. I will thank you several times in my thoughts and prayers.

Todd Jedrzejczyk

Themes: possessions, material goods, priorities

God of My Heart

"I saw all the deeds that are done under the sun; and see, all is vanity and a chasing after wind. What is crooked cannot be made straight, and what is lacking cannot be counted" (Ecclesiastes 1:14-15).

God of Direction,

Guide me on the path that I have chosen to live. You made each of us different, and my path will be different from those that others will choose. Let me rejoice in that difference. Sometimes it does all seem useless. I have followed my path and accomplished many things that I am proud of, but no matter how much I accomplish, I always want more. When I take a good, honest look at my life, I see that only one thing matters: your unconditional love.

God, I want to have a positive impact on other's lives. Help me to think deeply about the ways I choose to act and to consider carefully the things I choose to believe. Let me realize that I can't accomplish everything, but I can accomplish some things. Guide me on my way so I do not stumble off your path.

Today I will appreciate the differences I see around me and thank God for them.

Brandi Holys

Themes: accomplishments, differences, unconditional love

"As the blast of the trumpet grew louder and louder, Moses would speak and God would answer him in thunder" *(Exodus 19:19).*

God of Moderation,

I have been known to have a big mouth at times, and so I would appreciate a "nudge" when I need to keep it shut. When I get rowdy in class I later feel bad because of it, but at the time, being the center of attention seems more important than anything else. I thank you for giving me a strong voice, God, but I know sometimes I need to use it in a more constructive manner.

God, give me the sense to stay quiet when others are talking. Give me the grace I need to do that. Help me to see that sometimes my interruptions are inappropriate. I don't want to be hurtful or rude to my teachers or classmates.

Today I will think before I speak.

Jason Wenz

Themes: attention, self-discipline, speech

God of My Heart

"Do not fear for I am with you, do not be afraid for I am your God; I will strengthen you, I will help you, I will uphold you with my victorious right hand" (Isaiah 41:10).

God of My Strength,

I always end up trying to be so independent. I struggle to carry my burdens alone, especially the pain of death. Even when in my heart I know you can help me handle it, for some reason I hold back.

Please be with me. When troubles hit my life, give me the courage to carry on and face the day, knowing that you're helping me carry my burdens.

Today I will make the effort to talk to you if I'm stressed or hurting.

Sara Heim

Themes: death, troubles

"For love is strong as death, passion fierce as the grave. It's flashes are flashes of fire, a raging flame. Many waters cannot quench love, neither can floods drown it" (Song of Solomon 8:6b-7a).

God of Passion,

Love is powerful. Passion is strong, so strong that morals are forgotten. So many times we young people—and older people too—give in to passion before we really think about what we are doing —before we think about the consequences of our actions. Our passion is strong, but it can be controlled, because we, as human beings, have the gift of free will that gives us the power to make choices.

God, there have been times in my life when I have been flooded with passion, with the heat of the moment. Help me during these times to make the right decisions. I will not give in to passion because I know what is right and what is wrong. My body is mine and it is a gift from you. With your guidance, God, I will take care of my body and my soul.

Today I will think about the choices that I make and the consequences that might follow my choices.

Jenny Love

Themes: passion, choices, consequences, love

103

God of My Heart

"Then he said, 'Open the window eastward; and he opened it'"
(2 Kings 13:17a).

God of My Vision,

Last week I felt like true happiness was in my grasp, but it slipped away. Why can't I be hopeful that better things will happen? I've often heard it said, "When God closes a door, somewhere God opens a window." Where is the window I am looking for?

Please open my eyes to the goodness around me. Help me to realize that true happiness is being satisfied with my life and feeling love surround me.

Today I resolve to recognize the happy moments in my day.

Theresa Schneider

Themes: happiness, satisfaction, hope

"The cloud was seen overshadowing the camp" (Wisdom 19:7a).

God of Guidance,

I feel I am in this fog, floating along not really knowing what is going on. I feel friends are losing touch with me and I with them. Life is too hectic and too fast-paced. It's like I can see them, but I can't really hear them. I can't see their hurt or sense their feelings the way I used to. All I see right now is just a person and a face. I am even too busy to sit down and write letters. I feel the days sliding past and I do nothing to get through this cloud.

I try not to think about it, but I shut myself out from the world sometimes when what I really need to do is let people in. I feel I am missing something, but I don't know what it is. I want the feeling again of being wanted and needed. I want people to see me and not just hear me, and vice versa. I want to get out of this fog.

Today I will write at least one letter to a friend and work at improving my communication skills.

Pam Freeman

Themes: detachment, reaching out, busy-ness

God of My Heart

"As you therefore have received Christ Jesus the Lord, continue to live your lives in him, rooted and built up in him and established in the faith, just as you were taught, abounding in thanksgiving" (Colossians 2:6-7).

Faithful God,

So many things seem to take precedence over you in our lives. We skip weekly church in order to finish our homework, or we skip daily prayer time because it's just not convenient, or we're just too busy to pray right then. School, work and friends become more important than you, God. Of course, we know that's not right, but nonetheless it happens.

Help me, God, to put you first. Help me to look to you with thanks in the good times and for help through the bad times. Give me the strength to live fully for you and the courage to have your will at the root of my every action and intention. Help me put you, God, before everything else.

Today I will take time out to talk with you, God, and I will make you my first priority.

Lynn Smith

Themes: thanks, priorities

"Do not look at wine when it is red, when it sparkles in the cup and goes down smoothly. At the last it bites like a serpent, and stings like an adder... 'They struck me,' you will say, 'but I was not hurt. They beat me but I did not feel it. When shall I awake? I will seek another drink'" (Proverbs 23:31-32, 35).

God of Decision-Making,

As I was reading this scripture, it kind of surprised me that there were people who drank too much in the Bible. We hear so much today about alcohol and its effects, but even before the time of Jesus, there were people abusing alcohol and drinking too much.

God, help me to be wise in my decision-making and to stay away from parties or places where I know alcohol is present. Instead, I want to spend time with people who don't abuse alcohol and who don't drink. I know I will be a much healthier and happier person. Together we can make an impact on others. It's always easier to do the right thing if I know I have someone around who shares my views.

Today I will share my views on alcohol with a friend.

Jenny Love

Themes: decisions, alcohol

God of My Heart

"With my mouth I will give great thanks to the Lord; I will praise him in the midst of the throng" (Psalm 109:30).

Creator, God,

Please teach me to be grateful, to say thanks for the many things you have done for me and have given me. You put me on this earth for a reason. You love me. I want to learn to say thank you, even when things don't go my way. Teach me to appreciate you and your many gifts by respecting your creation.

Help me learn to care for your creation in as many ways as I can.

Today I will say a special thanks to you for the many things you have given me, especially the beauty and bounty of your creation. I will show my appreciation to you by doing some act to help keep our planet healthy.

Collette Willits

Themes: Thanksgiving, creation, gratefulness

"He has broken my strength in midcourse; he has shortened my days. 'Oh my God,' I say, 'do not take me away at the mid-point of my life...'" (Psalm 102:23-24a).

Strong God,

You have made us weak for a reason. When we are tempted to have a drink of beer or to have a smoke we are naturally weak, but if we turn away from these evils then our weakness turns to strength. Allow me to grow old, not so that I may become wealthy or famous, but so I may turn as much of my weakness into strength as possible.

When I feel life getting to be a heavy burden on my shoulders, help me to visualize people that I know who have lived long, fruitful lives in your presence. They carry your words in their minds and your actions in their hearts.

Today I will visit an older person and listen to the wisdom they are willing to share with me

Matt Voss

Themes: weakness, strength, aging, wisdom

God of My Heart

"Sing praises to the Lord with the lyre, with the lyre and the sound of melody" (Psalm 98:5).

God of Music,

Music is such an important part of all of our lives. We all have certain types that we like and certain types we can't stand. But every human being listens to music and enjoys it or is relaxed by it.

What would life be like without music? I can't imagine how I would be able to relax, block out noise or enjoy my life without music. There would be no MTV, Omaha Opera, Christmas carols, Beethoven symphonies, Pachelbel Canons, Poison, Extreme, Tesla, Mariah Carey...need I say more? I didn't think so.

Today, God, when I need to relax, I will put in my favorite tape or CD, then listen, relax and thank you for making human beings capable of composing and enjoying music.

Sarah Swanson

Themes: music, relaxing, joy

"Rain in abundance, O God, you showered abroad; you restored your heritage when it languished" (Psalm 68:9).

God of All Seasons,

Everything you have given me is beautiful. I am in awe at the majesty of your world. I feel privileged to witness such grand miracles as the grace of a forest turning to radiant glory in the tinted autumn. New, green life bursting forth every year against all odds is just as amazing to me as changing water into wine. I watch the trees as the seasons come and go each year and admire your work.

If I learn your lessons well I shall be able to serve you as the trees do by nurturing the gifts and talents you have given me. I too shall blossom.

Today I will think about the lesson you teach us through nature and the changing seasons.

Libby Halley

Themes: seasons, nature, miracles

God of My Heart

"God is our refuge and strength, a very present help in trouble. Therefore we will not fear, though the earth should change, though the mountains shake in the heart of the sea" (Psalm 46:1-2).

Eternal Friend,

I don't need a scripture to tell me that you are always here, constantly guiding and protecting me whenever I call your name. I do sometimes wonder, though, if you are here for me in order to make my life go smoothly, or if you are here in order to calm me down when it feels like the end of the world and I am afraid.

I don't know what I'd do without your constant hand on my shoulder. I believe you are here with me. I believe that you give me a chance to live so many different experiences every day. Words aren't enough to express my love and gratitude toward everything you have done for me! I know that reaching out to others will help me overcome my own depression and fears, and show my appreciation to you, too.

Today, even if I'm feeling down, I will go out of my way to help someone else.

Ann Larsen

Themes: reaching out, God's presence

"Contend, O Lord, with those who contend with me; fight against those who fight against me!" (Psalm 35:1).

God of Power,

I don't know how to put up with people when they anger me. I need to control my anger and I need to learn to judge everyone fairly. I appreciate your understanding and kindness in helping me deal with this.

Anger is a powerful emotion and it can control me. Help me not to let it run my life. Help me use it's power rarely and wisely. I know it has the potential to be a positive force in my life.

Today I will work on channeling my anger.

Paul Gilg

Theme: anger

God of My Heart

"The Lord is my light and my salvation; whom shall I fear? The Lord is the stronghold of my life; of whom shall I be afraid?" (Psalm 27:1).

Protective God,

It's hard to make moral decisions. Sometimes I want to do things that I know are not right. When times get stressful in school and I have a lot on my mind, I feel alone and afraid inside, and that makes the decisions even harder.

Most of the time I try to do my best, but help me get through the other times when I'm not trying so hard. I know that you will give me the light I need when I feel surrounded by the dark. I know you will help me make good choices if I only ask for your help.

Today I will make the best moral decisions I can. I will trust in you, God, to be with me when I'm making them.

Jamie Hinde

Themes: moral decisions, stress

"Oh guard my life, and deliver me; do not let me be put to shame" (Psalm 25:20a).

Giver of Life,

I've been thinking lately about my grades. My parents put a lot of weight on them. Somehow they aren't as important to me as they are to them. I do know that they're right when they say I don't always work up to my potential, even though I don't admit it to them.

Please help me to use the gifts you have given me to complete my studies. Aid me in my school work and in my self-discipline. Thank you for giving me the opportunity to be who I am and to have parents that care about me. I promise to do my best to use the gifts you have given me and to work up to my potential.

Today, I will do my homework before participating in any other activities.

Chris Lyster

Themes: potential, grades, gifts, studies

God of My Heart

"To you, O Lord, I lift up my soul. O my God, in you I trust; do not let me be put to shame; do not let my enemies exult over me" (Psalm 25:1-2).

God of Guidance,

During the last couple of months I've been worried about what I am going to do with my life. I am bored. Nothing sounds exciting anymore, and time just keeps flying by.

Help me to rediscover excitement in my life and to know that you are in the midst of it all. I want to rediscover your love for me, as well. Please hear my prayer.

Today I will take time to pray.

Joe Johnson

Themes: boredom, prayer, intimacy with God

"I beat them fine, like dust before the wind; I cast them out like the mire of the streets" (Psalm 18:42).

God of My Life,

Many times in my life I do not give people the respect they deserve. Although I may not trample them down physically, I often do so with words or actions.

Help me to realize that we are all your people. I am not a better person because I am stronger or smarter than someone else.

Today I will be respectful of people. I will empathize with other's feelings. I will say "Hi" to someone who looks discouraged, and I will attempt to brighten their day.

Brian Harvat

Themes: respect, pride

God of My Heart

"For who is God except the Lord? And who is a rock besides our God?—the God who girded me with strength, and made my way safe" (Psalm 18:31-32).

God of My Journey,

You have often protected me from accidents which could have lead to real tragedy. You have helped me in this way through all my car crashes, and I have come out of them safely. Even I am amazed! I could have been seriously injured more than once. Thank you for keeping me safe in my travels. Give me the good sense to be more cautious.

Today I ask that you protect me, my family and my friends as we go travel in our cars.

Today I will be a safe driver and make a habit of wearing my seat-belt.

Shelly Byrne

Themes: safety, driving, protection

"Just as water reflects the face, so one human heart reflects another" (Proverbs 27:19).

God of Beauty,

So many times I criticize my physical appearance. I either look too tired, too fat, too blah or too dumpy. Accepting compliments is something I rarely do well, because I fail to see in myself what they proclaim. I am very rarely satisfied with the way I look and have a hard time believing people's compliments. I tend to get tied up in the perfection of my physical appearance and fail to appreciate my real beauty.

Help me to realize, God, that internal beauty is more important than physical perfection. Help me to accept myself for who I am and not for who I wish I were or what I wish I looked like.

Today I will graciously accept all compliments that come my way.

Michelle Hinze

Themes: physical appearance, compliments, beauty

119

God of My Heart

"If your enemies are hungry, give them bread to eat; and if they are thirsty, give them water to drink; for you will heap coals of fire upon their heads, and the Lord will reward you" (Proverbs 25:21-22).

Kind God,

You teach us to be generous to everyone we meet, even our enemies. I do try to be generous and to love my neighbor as myself, but it is so hard to do most of the time. When I see someone that needs something, I do try to be friendly and help them out. If they need lunch money or need help moving something and I am able to help, I do.

Give me the grace I need to be generous, God. I have so much, I want to share. I want to follow your word and become a friend even to my enemies.

Today I will begin by treating those I consider my enemies with respect, even though we obviously disagree.

Don Steffes

Themes: enemies, respect

"All our steps are ordered by the Lord; how then can we understand our own ways?" (Proverbs 20:24).

Lord of Laughter,

I am worried and scared of what's to come. The unknown is always frightening.

You are peace for the frightened. Grant me confidence in knowing that you will be with me so I have no reason to be afraid.

Today I will laugh and rejoice, knowing I can count on you for direction on my journey.

Tim Murphy

Themes: confidence, journey, fear, peace

God of My Heart

"Some friends play at friendship, but a true friend sticks closer than one's nearest kin" (Proverbs 18:24).

My True Friend,

You are always here for me. When I'm down and out and feel like there is no one to turn to, you are here. I can tell you anything, and you always listen, no matter how busy you are. Thank you.

God, please guide me to choose friends that will be good for me. Help me to develop the qualities needed to be a faithful companion to others. Thank you for your undying friendship.

Today I will show my friends that I appreciate them. I will thank them for the times they have been there for me.

Rachel Mullen

Theme: friends

"Precious treasure remains in the house of the wise, but the fool devours it" (Proverbs 21:20).

God of the Earth,

Today I pray for our world, for every tree, flower, grain of sand and fish in the sea. We hurt our world so badly with our "miracle" chemicals and our "greed for profit." Every day, we burn acres of rain forest. Water cannot be used in its natural form, and the air is polluted and blocks out the stars at night. Disease runs rampant, and the land weeps from misuse.

Help us, God, to wake up and see what we are doing. We need to admit that our greed and carelessness destroys our earth. I do hope your final plan is to save our earth.

Today I will begin my new world effort. I will work harder to recycle and not litter.

Carrie McCraw

paper   aluminum   glass

Themes: pollution, greed, creation

God of My Heart

"There is a way that seems right to a person, but its end is the way to death. Even in laughter the heart is sad, and the end of joy is grief" (Proverbs 14:12-13).

Gracious Spirit,

Dealing with death can be very difficult. Recently I experienced the loss of my grandmother. I know it is better for Grandma to be in heaven with you—she's not suffering any more—but my heart still aches. I know she will always be with me in my heart, and her spirit lives on, but I really miss her.

Thank you, God, for helping me and my family through this troubled time. Help me to be open to the needs of others who have experienced the death of a loved one. None of us escape the pain that death brings, but we can help each other get through it. It's a real gift of love.

Today I will reach out to others that I see are hurting.

Molly Swanson

Themes: death, reaching out

"The heart knows its own bitterness, and no stranger shares its joy" (Proverbs 14:10).

Trusting God,

So many times in my life I have felt alone, like nobody else knew what I was feeling or what I was going through. It is awful to be so lonely when surrounded by so many people. Sometimes I have a problem and I feel like I have no one to turn to for help.

Help me, God, to realize that even though people might not understand exactly what I am feeling, they are willing to listen. Help me also to be more expressive, so that when I have a problem or a bad day, I have somewhere to turn.

Today I will reach out and share some of my feelings with a person I can trust.

Michelle Perlinger

Themes: loneliness, sharing, trust

God of My Heart

"A faithful witness does not lie, but a false witness breathes out lies" (Proverbs 14:5).

God of Good Choices,

As we go through life, we are often dishonest with people in the things we do: school work, friendships and family relationships. This dishonesty shows our disrespect for you, God, as well as for ourselves. By cheating our way through life and not using our potential, we say that we have no reverence for you and the gifts you have given us.

God, I need help to let my daily actions reflect my identity as a Christian. I want to show that I do have reverence for you and respect for myself. Let me be less influenced by others who are dishonest. Growing in my faith and working at being honest can only make me happier and bring me closer to you.

Today I will be honest in all my dealings with people.

Jerome Gollihare

Themes: honesty, choices, self-respect

126

"The appetite of the lazy craves, and gets nothing, while the appetite of the diligent is richly supplied" (Proverbs 13:4).

Gracious God,

Sometimes I don't work hard enough on projects. At other times I work very hard and put my heart into it, and still I don't get that much out of it. Those times when I am lazy and expect to be rewarded I know I am letting myself down.

Two areas in which I feel disappointment after having worked hard are in my grades and in sports. When I get a low grade or when we lose in sports I feel I haven't gotten anything out of my hard work. Somewhere in the back of my head, though, I still have hope that in the long run my effort will pay off.

God, please help me to always do my best and not to be a lazy person that just wants things handed to them. Help and guide me to be independent except when help is needed.

Today I will not give up on my studies nor on my desire to improve my skills.

Monica Manning

Themes: hard work, improvement, studies

God of My Heart

"Do not enter the path of the wicked, and do not walk in the way of evildoers" (Proverbs 4:14).

Forgiving One,

There are times in my life when I think bad thoughts. I know that they are wrong, and I am sorry.

Please forgive me for those thoughts. I know I am a wonderful person because you made me. Please help me not to think such negative thoughts. I want to continue becoming the good person you mean for me to be.

Today I will think only good thoughts in hopes that it will become a habit.

Anne Petersen

Themes: bad thoughts, attitude

"The fear of the Lord is the beginning of knowledge; fools despise wisdom and instruction" (Proverbs 1:7).

Persevering God,

Studying can be difficult. There are times when I want to say, "The heck with it," and give up all hope of learning something.

When I am studying for a test or taking one, help me through it. Please give me perseverance to use the knowledge that I've gained through hours of study. Give me the strength to carry on after a rough day of school and my other activities. Help me use my talents wisely, God, for I know they will be challenged.

Today I will be glad that I have a capacity for learning. I will be thankful for school and my teachers.

Chris Anderson

Themes: studies, talents, perseverance

God of My Heart

"My child, do not forget my teaching, but let your heart keep my commandments" (Proverbs 3:1).

God of My Heart,

During grade school one of the first things I had to memorize was the Ten Commandments. I memorized them, but never took the time to understand their meaning. My teachers were trying to get the Commandments not only into my mind, but also into my heart. The heart is where the Commandments are truly lived. I'm starting to understand that now.

Help me, God, to keep your Commandments and to appreciate the goodness and order they bring to our world.

Today I will use the Ten Commandments in my decision making, whether it be about going to church or showing respect for my parents.

Matt Irish

Themes: Ten Commandments, obedience

"Keep hold of instruction; do not let go; guard her, for she is your life" (Proverbs 4:13).

God of Knowledge,

Why do we make fun of what we don't understand? If we could see the true meaning in things, we probably wouldn't be so quick to judge. Sometimes we laugh because we are embarrassed or immature. I remember in grade school when they taught sex education. We all laughed because we didn't know how to handle such a serious subject.

What do I laugh at now? Why do I laugh? Do I look for the true meaning? Am I growing in maturity and trying to understand people and things that are different than what I am used to? Laughing at people and things often shows my ignorance—my lack of instruction.

Today I will take the time to understand. I will not laugh at people or things just because they are different.

Amy Jones

Themes: laughter, maturity, differences

Scripture Index

Scripture Index

Scripture Index

Scripture Index

Theme Index

Theme Index

Theme Index

Theme Index

Theme Index

Theme Index

More praise for *God of My Heart...*

"Immersed in scripture, especially those psalms, and practiced in rituals of word and table, Catholics gradually discover how to live and how to speak. This book is a glimpse of that learning: not always smooth, not always polished, but always striving. The words of these young people should encourage us all to keep the conversation going."

—*Gabe Huck*
Liturgy Training Publications

For teens and their parents who want just the right words to address God, this is a great start. We should never underestimate the prayer life of teens. It's often their best way to deal with the trials and troubles—as well as the joys—that are part of their often-difficult lives."

—*Dr. David M. Thomas*
Graduate Professor of Community
Leadership and Family Regis University

"A collection of remarkable prayers straight from the lives and growing-up experiences of teenagers. If you are looking for a daily prayer in the classroom, a weekly prayer for the youth group, a monthly prayer to post on the family refrigerator door, or a flip-through-and-look resource for personal reflection, here is the book for you!"

—*Lisa Calderone-Stewart*
Associate Director for the Office of Schools,
Child and Youth Ministries
Archdiocese of Milwaukee

"I relate to these prayers on a very personal level which is incredible. Very down-to-earth and comprehensive. Receiving this has truly been a God-send."

—*Amber Spradlin*
12th grader